FOUR GERMAN POETS

GÜNTER EICH
HILDE DOMIN
ERICH FRIED
GÜNTER KUNERT

FOUR GERMAN POETS

GÜNTER EICH
HILDE DOMIN
ERICH FRIED
GÜNTER KUNERT

Translated and edited by
Agnes Stein

Red Dust/New York/1979

Printed in the United States of America.
Library of Congress Catalogue Card Number 78-59474
ISBN: 0-87376-034-4

This publication has been supported in part by grants from the National En-
dowment for the Arts in Washington, D.C., a Federal agency; and from the
New York State Council on the Arts.

Translator's Dedication:
For George

Acknowledgements

For permission to translate the following poems acknowledgements and thanks are due to: Carl Hanser Verlag, Munich, for 'Dream Talk', 'Recurrent Dreams', and 'Deep Dream' by Erich Fried from *Warngedichte* (copyright 1964); 'Birth of a Mermaid', 'Two Laughing Soldiers from St. Pauli', and 'Love Song' by Erich Fried from *Zeitfragen* (copyright 1968); 'House Calls', 'The Last House', 'I Call Stop Thief', 'Berlin Afternoon', 'The Other Side of the Styz', 'Romantic Poem', 'Sometimes Smoke', 'The Way', 'Trickery of Enemies', 'Schiller's Bed', and 'Proposal' by Günter Kunert from *Warnung Vor Spiegelin* (copyright 1974); 'Poor Consolation', 'Introjective Poem', 'Days and Days', 'Bitter Poem', 'Glance in the Mirror', 'The Rustling of Rain', 'The Neighbor', 'Signs—Berlin Style', 'Berlin Dance of Death', 'Remembering IV', and 'Conjunctive Double' by Günter Kunert from *Im Weiteren Fortgang* (copyright 1974); Claassen Verlag, Dusseldorf, for 'At the Rest Stops' and 'Inscription' by Erich Fried from *Reich der Steine* (copyright 1963); 'Defeat', 'Pause', 'To the Watering Hole', 'In the Forest', 'Looking Backward', and 'Decrees' by Erich Fried from *Befreiung von der Flucht* (copyright 1968); S. Fischer Verlag, Frankfurt, for 'Landscape in Motion' and 'Cautious Hope' by Hilde Domin from *Nur Eine Rose Als Stütze* (copyright 1959, 1977); 'Traveling Light', 'April', 'Autumn Eyes', 'Not To Be Stopped', 'Song of Encouragement II', and 'Arranging Manuscripts' by Hilde Domin from *Rückkehr der Schiffe* (copyright 1962); 'Cologne', 'Remigration', 'Anxiety', 'Do Not Grow Weary',

Contents

Introduction

After 1945 we expect certain directions in German poetry of the past to have disappeared. At this war's ending it would have been difficult for any poet to resound with romantic echoes or hark back nostalgically to those most famous of yearning lines, Goethe's "Über allen Gipfeln ist Ruh." That "Ruh" was now gone. The world lay in pieces and, in the progression of worldwide events, reached a fragmentation expressed by Gottfried Benn as "Die Welt ist zerdacht"—the world has been thought into fragments. Ideologies took their toll, technology its share. Rationalism and positivism, the strongholds of the conceptual mind, lay shattered.

Although some post-war poets retreated into mysticism and romantic naturalism there were others who retained their hold on a cultural consciousness. Among these, Eich, Domin, Fried and Kunert are four who went forward in new directions. They kept their vision sharp and clear on the world around them. Living in different times and places each of these poets developed his individual style: Eich is the most present-place conscious and the most melancholic in tone; Fried's social outrage forges the sharpest tongue; Domin generalizes the pain of exile to extend it to the human condition, the loneliness of the human spirit in a bureaucratic and technological world, while keeping a keen eye on the walls that threaten to separate the individual from a common humanity, Kunert also explores the existential human condition. For none of these poets does politics win over poetry. They are craftsmen and are devoted as any poet to the "game of language" as Auden put it—only for them it is to be played with counters that bear the mark of the world which has given them shape.

These poets share a language which is contemporary German and a context which is the Western world. They are continuing a fight against those forces that threaten dehumanization: unjust wars, violence, bureaucratic cant, technological mechanization, wherever they manifest themselves and regardless of the political situation.

Sometimes it is hard to distinguish an existential despair from the pessimism induced by prevailing social conditions. This pessimism is strong in Eich, the earliest of them. His awareness of the immediate environment may remind us of Rilke's involvement with nature. For Eich the natural surroundings are a familiar presence, but one that often fills him with unrest. The rain seems to be drumming out messages meant for him, and as he views the Oder, his river, he sees the dark as it was before creation.

Eich sends postcards. Palmyra, Paris, Vancouver, the prospects vaguely threaten:

Old Post Card 10

Why was the coffee
not drunk
Despite the floods
we were sitting well,
had rented boats between
the trees of the boulevard.
Why did the sugar
not dissolve?
Nothing came to a finish.

One suspects the danger may be man-made. "Wake up, your dreams are bad!" he cries. Opt for discomfort, be sand, not oil in the works of the world, his message reads. On the jacket of the collection his wife, Ilse Aichinger, made after his death, there is this quote:

No longer shall we be settlers,
we shall teach our daughters and sons the
    language of the iguana,
and commit ourselves to disorder.
the world has failed our friends.

Today Hilde Domin is as much concerned with the present state of the world as with her past experience of exile. In an essay she claims that the return to her homeland plays a stronger role in her poetry than that of exile. But the return, she modifies, must be considered in the context of exile. Moreover there is a sense in which exile is the human condition at its extremity—namely when consciousness is threatened with the separation of its subjective-objective poles. Social forces that demand a dogmatic adherence to their rules and conventions make for such a split. This is the condition of the exile when he is forced to accomodate himself to the host's way of life. Against these binding structures, intellectual as well as social, Domin takes a stand.

This is not to say that she herself writes with a programmatic direction. Usefulness, she has said, grows in the poem on its way from author to reader. A poem that begins as a love lyric may become a political message in its later significance. The "use" she values in poetry is the awareness it gives the reader of his "singular identity." To maintain that we need a clear eye and an honest voice:

This is our freedom
to name the right names
without fear
with a small voice.

Erich Fried is outspoken, direct and does not hesitate to attack the injustice, as he sees it, of a particular issue. But his critical spirit plays a larger, more generalized role. In a Note to *Aufforderung Zur Unruhe,* published in 1970, he has this to say:

> The raised forefinger did not stand as godfather to these poems, rather the hollow feeling on waking or in tossing sleeplessly, the unlocalized anxiety, the shaken head, fear or pity, or the bitterness at the sudden insight into the connections between various news reports. No, these poems are not warnings in the sense of products of a doctrinaire world view or of a political party. Nor are these concepts or images which I would wish to press on others, at the most these were pressed on me, when old thought categories and age old prejudices forced a shudder at the sight of glittering, new as nails weaponry...

In 1974 Fried published *Gegengift*—antidotes to pretension, illusion, delusion, lies, and sometimes it seems, hope itself.

Günter Kunert writes with the premise that poetry has a direction and function which is neither narrowly political nor thoughtlessly academic. When he speaks in his poetry he says something, but for himself and his fellow human beings, and not in the service of a cause. One can read traces of Brecht in his humor, but it is not the sort that can be restricted by ideology. The genial irony of Günter Grass is evident as a prose parellel.

Themes which run through his poetry are given a paradoxical definition: the joy of life encounters pain of death; irrelevance of power meets the significance of the individual. The poem, he has said, is language before it functions as terminology, a relative autonomous image of consciousness. We see life and art reinforcing each other:

> My poems are my poems: expressions of my self, a self
> which may later be seen as a print of time and society.
> I write according to my art and manner, in my script,"
> by which is meant style. One strives for a distinctive
> style in order to hypothesize a distinctive view of the
> world. Literature, as a whole, is necessary as an aid to
> life.*

This assertion might have the agreement of all four of the poets selected for this volume.

*"Das Bewusstsein des Gedichts" from *Warum Schreiben* (Berlin und Weimar 1976)

GÜNTER EICH

Günter Eich was born in 1907 in Lebus on the Oder, a village not far from Berlin. He died in 1972. While serving in the German Army in World War II, Eich was taken prisoner of war. This experience is reflected in the poems "Inventory," and "Latrine."

Although his first volume of poetry was published in 1930 Eich's recognition as a writer did not come until after the war with the publication of *Abgelegene Gehöfte* (*Deserted Farmyards*) in 1948. This volume was followed by *Untergrund Bahn* (*Underground Train*) in 1949, and *Botschaft Des Regens* (*Rain Messages*) in 1955.

Hans Enzensberger[1] speaks of the not unexpected literary silence Germany experienced after the war. Through perverted usage the German language itself lay destroyed by the Hitler rabble. The first to again make their voices heard with any strength were Bertolt Brecht and Gottfried Benn. At opposite ends of the political spectrum they were united in carrying on the pre-war expressionistic tradition.

The romanticism of the "nature lyric" had made it the only form acceptable to the Nazis. After the war it was used by some poets as a shallow yet safe escape from the present scene. While the philosopher Theodor W. Adorno stated that to go on writing lyric poetry after Auschwitz was barbaric, the lyric tradition could not be entirely dismissed. After all there had been Rilke shining with the reflected glow of his angelic guardians. A pre-war

---

[1] Enzensberger, Hans. *In Search of a Lost Language*, *Encounter*, Vol. XXI, iii, 1963.

poet Rilke sang of time, death and God and rejoiced in the consciousness of self. And it was as a lyric poet that Günter Eich found his voice. But Rilke's angels were no longer there for Eich who wrote of time and death as centered in man's consciousness, leaving him destitute and alone.

Eich gave the "naturlyrik" a new direction, a new dignity and intelligence. His poems mirror the real world and reflect its social evils. Their personal consciousness which the nature themes support is not completely isolated from the social, witness: "Dreams," "As Gray as the Rain May Be," "Look at the Fingertips," among others. His social criticism has a melancholy tone and is washed with humor.

The poems are sparse. Someone describes them in terms of oriental brush paintings. Isolated fragments are bound together with a collage effect. The soft tones and the fragile touch do not hide the hard sense of the content.

INVENTORY

This is my cap,
this is my coat,
here my shaving stuff
in the cotton sack.

Tin cans
my plate, my mug.
I've scratched
my name in the tin.

Scratched with this
precious nail
which I hide
from envious eyes.

In my bread bag
you'll find a pair
of woolen socks and a few
things I won't tell anyone.

At night it serves
as a pillow for my head,
cardboard that comes between
me and the earth.

Most of all
I love my pencil
during the day it writes
verses composed at night.

This is my notebook,
this my tent-cloth,
this is my towel,
this is my thread.

LATRINE

Over the stinking ditch
paper soaked blood and urine,
flies shining and buzzing,
I sit crouched on my knees.

The view to the wooded shore,
gardens, the beached boat,
gravelled dirt sliding
in the waste water froth.

Ringing wildly in my ears
is the poetry of Hölderlin,
like pure white snow clouds
now mirrored in urine.

"Now go and greet
the beautiful Garonne ..."
Below stumbling footsteps
clouds swim away at a run.

DREAMS

Wake up, your dreams are bad!
Stay awake, the horror is coming closer.

It will reach even you who live far distant
 from the cities where blood is flowing,
even you taking that afternoon nap
which you don't care to have disturbed.
If not today, it will come tomorrow,
be assured.

"Oh pleasant sleep
on pillows embroidered with red flowers,
A Christmas present from Anita on which
 she worked for three weeks,
oh, pleasant sleep
when the roast was juicy and the vegetables tender.
Falling asleep you recalled last night's
 TV review of the week:
Spring lambs, nature awakening, the opening
 of the Casino at Baden-Baden,
Cambridge beating Oxford by two and a half lengths—
enough to occupy the mind.

Oh this soft pillow of first class down!
on which you can forget the annoying disturbances
 of this world, this news report for instance:
The defendant accused of performing an abortion
said in her defense:
The woman, mother of seven children
 came to me with a suckling babe
for whom she had no diapers so that she
 wrapped it in newspapers.
Well, this is the business of the court,
 not ours,

What can we do about it when
life is tougher for one person than for another,
and as for the future, let our
        grandchildren fight it out."

"Ah, you're already asleep? Wake sharp,
        my friend!
The waters have already risen inside
        the enclosures and the posts are manned."

No, do not sleep as long as the
        authorities of the world are busy!
Mistrust their powers which they claim
        to have won in the struggle for your sakes!
Do the useless, sing the songs one does
        not expect to come out of your mouths,
be the sand, disturbing, not the oil
        in the world's machinery!

AS GRAY AS THE RAIN MAY BE

As gray as the rain may be
the woods have a yellow look.
Ah, whatever happens to me
are things I myself evoke.

The power of poems,
the intimate embraces,
the night full of talk,
summer's stream races.

The magic of verse
in hunger forgotten,
those tender hearts,
who now regrets them?

Loyal companions
for so long buried,
the rains of autumn
for me are hurried.

RAIN MESSENGERS

News, meant for me,
drummed onwards from one rain to another,
dragged, like a sickness,
from slate roof to tile,
smuggled goods, brought to someone
who never wanted them—

Tin window frames ring outside the wall,
rattling letters that join each other,
the rain speaking
a language which I believed
no one but me understood—

Dismayed I take in
messages of despair,
messages of poverty
and messages of blame.
It pains me that these are addressed to me
who does not believe himself guilty.

I'll say it aloud
I'm not afraid of rain and its accusations
nor of him who sent them on to me.
At the right time
I'll go out and answer him.

IN THE SUNLIGHT

The sun as it chances
copper and gold
flickering the sleeper—
I did not ask for it.

I don't want it or the way it tans my skin
and does me good,
I fear luck—
I did not ask for it.

You who take it,
copper and gold
that it may harden the kernels of wheat,
that it may cook the grape—
who are you that you are not afraid?

What condescending it gave,
what we took without thought,
the gift unrequested—
one overwhelming day
a return will be demanded.

The allowable waste,
the copper small change,
the heaps of gold,
the dissipated riches, an exact
return will be demanded.
But our pockets will be empty,
and the creditor is unmerciful.
How shall we ever pay?
O brother, are you not afraid?

END OF SUMMER

Who can live without the consolation of trees!

How good that they take their part in dying!
The peaches are harvested, the plums getting their color,
while time rushes beneath the arched bridge.

I confide my despair to the passage of birds.
Calmly it measures its share of eternity.
Its stretch
becomes visible as a dark force in the pattern of leaves,
the movement of wings colors the fruit.

Be patient.
Soon the bird script will be decoded,
beneath your tongue the taste of a copper penny.

PRESENCE

The poplars of the Leopoldstrasse
seen on different days
but always autumnal,
always ghosts of a clouded sun
or the weavings of rain.

Where are you when you walk next to me?

Always ghosts of displaced times,
past and yet to come:
the life in caves,
the eternal troglodyte times,
the bitter taste of the Heliogabolus pillars
and that of the Hotel St. Moritz.
Gray holes, barracks,
where luck begins,
this gray luck.

The pressure of your arm answering me,
the archipelago, island chains, finally sand banks,
only reverberations
from sweetness of union.
(But you are of my blood,
over these stones, next to the shrubbery
old men at rest on the fixed benches
and the rattling of trolley line No. 6,
anemone, present
with the force of water in the eye
and the moisture of lips—)

And always specters spinning around us,
dissolving the present,
invalid love,
the proof of our accidental nature,

the sparse green on the poplar trees,
and as calculated by the city fathers,
autumn in the gutters
and the questions of fortune answered.

WHERE I LIVE

When I opened the window
fish swam into the room,
herring. It seemed
a swarm was passing by.
They even played between the pear trees.
But most
kept to the woods,
over the fenced trees and gravel pits.

They're annoying. But more annoying
are the sailors
(those of higher ranks, pilots, captains as well),
who often come to the open window
and ask for a light for their bad tobacco.

I'm going to move.

MIDDAY ROUND TWO

The gray tip of the pastor
at the sacristy door.
Across his blinded eyes
the wings of sparrows swirling in sand.

Like memories he senses
the leash for the peacock flock
that looked like a break in the cemetery wall,
the heaving of gravestones
when the caterpillar hunches at the crippling sting,
the bricks discoloring
at the scream of a dying mole.

Calmly he notes
the rumors from the woods,
the gates of Paradise are to be opened.

CHANGED LANDSCAPE

Depression comes out of the South
so that we see fields of snow
and the bare woods,
forgotten places
of the heart,
groves of doubt,
the weaving ways of care
and the fences of poverty.

Whether the dead note the South wind
is shown by the brackish fields.
(It differs
as the remains of snow differ).
The news mole mounds give
will spread,
but the village names
are no longer valid.

HERRENCHIEM SEE

All you wings of autumn
bird wind, bird leaves—
the grapes have been gathered,
snow is falling in the mountains.

Ludwig would not let anyone watch him eat.
The South wind runs into invisible dungeons,
but how easily the whirl of falling
sycamore leaves explains everything.

Rain beginning in the woods
reaches the table of the King,
in the pipes the bells of grazing cows,
so that he stops his ears with wax.
Behind keyholes servants laugh.

All you wings of autumn,
black leaves at twilight,
when the first windows shine
with despairing light,
when I hear my child's laugh,
and hide my eyes behind my hands.

SHORTLY BEFORE RAIN

It's going to rain, take the wash in!
Clothes pins are swaying on the line.
A cloud's shadow darkens the stone.
The roofs are full of thoughts.

They are thought in shingle and tile,
caulked chimneys and stinging smoke.
My eyes hear the dismaying words—
Oh silent speech from the burning bush!

A sob is beginning to rise in me.
Wandering shadows alter the stone.
Wind tears at the fluttering shirts.
It's going to rain, take the wash in!

THE GREAT LÜBBE-SEE

Cranes, flight of birds,
as I think about them,
the frame of a triangulated point.

Here it reached me,
with the dark wall of hills on the opposite shore,
the beginning of loneliness,
the wink of an eye
not to be borne a second time,
pigeon-eye with its soft reproach,
when the knife cuts its throat,
the beginning of loneliness,
here without bridge or boat,
the ledge of despair,
the triangulation point,
measurements made within nothingness
while bird flight unfolds itself,
windless September day,
a golden quickness flying off
on the wings of cranes,
leaving no trace.

POND IN DECEMBER

1

The green tuft of water plants,
the current
combing stones into their forehead.
Thoughts
icing the water.

2

Lines of ice ridges signal unrest,
reed fever, earthquake of snails,
we await the graphs.

3

The oil blob flows off like a boat,
the fishing-rod's shadow is forgotten.
Current, insight of fish.

VOYAGE

You can turn off
the leper's rattle,
close window and ears
and wait for him to pass.

But once you have heard it
you'll always hear it,
and because he won't go away
you must go.

Pack a bag, one not too heavy
because nobody will help carry it.
Steal away quietly and leave the door open,
you won't come back.

Go as far as you like to be rid of him,
take a boat or find a wilderness,
the leper's rattle will not quiet.

You'll take it along, if he stays behind.
Listen! how the drum roll pounds
with your own heart-beat.

LWOW

1

City sitting on how many hills,
a graying yellow.
A sound of bells goes with you,
heard in the clang
of your distinctive token.

2

Cliffs uncountable as fear.
The trolley ends
in a steppe of weeds
at torn-down gates.

LOOK AT THE FINGERTIPS

Look at the fingertips, at their discoloration!

One day it will return, the scrubbed out plague.
The postman will throw it like a letter into the
      rattling post box,
like a portion of herring it will lie on your plate,
a mother will give it, like her breast, to her child.

What shall we do now that no one is still alive
who knew how to deal with it?
Those on friendly terms with the abominable,
can await its visit in peace.
We continue to point towards good fortune
but it sits badly in our chairs.

Look at the fingertips! By the time they're black
it will be too late.

ODER, MY RIVER

1
Oder, my river
which has no source:
Drops trickle out
of the mountains of time,
water, tasting of childhood.

Oder, my river,
not too broad for shouting Hallos! across,
a November for rain.

Veil drawn across turnip fields,
meadow and mountain shore indistinguishable,
voices on the Bühnen and Treidel ways,
near unkempt pastures and reeds,
bells out of Frankfort and legends of the Reitweiner hills,
the ferry at Lebus and the house
on the right of the Oder where I was born,
the smithy in Podelzig and the tales
of my grandmother, who saw Sternickel, the murderer,
distance passes by in boats,
indifferently, with a flag flying at the mast.

Restlessness, with calm days or windy,
something special in the sound of clocks,
meal of wood-worm a hieroglyphic,
fires in the farmyard ovens,
dissatisfaction drowned in booze.
He comes, soon leaves again.
In Küstrin Friedrich saw Katte beheaded.
In Freienwalde Fontane visited his father.
The house is destroyed
where Kleist spent his childhood.

Unrest in field furrows and elderbush,
the incomprehensible in the heart.
Perfection does not thrive,
here no one binds the unruly into noble proportions,
and the dark is as before creation
undifferentiated from light.

2

Over my river
moon and constellations sit as everywhere.
The same wind from country to country
drives dust to pasture,
water has its fish,
air its birds.
The world was not named here.
But here hours were changed into water,
my years grew as grass,
houses were built out of moments.
Here farewell and return make their home,
here time becomes resident
like a lodger too poor
to move. He remains.

Yet a floating log,
a moving pile of sand,
scales of fish and a human hair,
my river will take swiftly in its flow
towards three estuaries, the sea and salt.

THE BROTHERS GRIMM

Burning nettle bush.
The burnt children
wait behind cellar windows.
The parents have left
saying they would soon return.

First came the wolf, who
brought the buns,
the hyena lent the spade,
the scorpion the TV program.

Outside the nettles are burning
without flames.
The parents have been gone a long time.

(The German "brenn" carries a double meaning: sting and burn.
Properly translated the "brennessel" is a stinging nettle, but this
would lose the double entendre which the "verbrannte" children
requires. Editor's note)

WHOOOO!

Where the lights begin
I remain invisible.
You won't read me in letters
and I hide myself in poems.

I gave you all
the last blow.
You won't meet me any more
no matter how long I call.

CONTINUING THE CONVERSION

1

Remembering the Dead

I remarked
that remembering is a form of forgetting.

It means
seeking flames in ashes,
doing geology in the rejected
deposits of the moment,
recreating the flow of time
from its insoluble chemistry.
It means:
separating the critique of bird flight
from the forenoon shopping
and the expectation of love.
Going there
where parallel lines intersect.
Fulfilling demands
of logic with dreams.
Removing fossils from glass cases,
dissolving them with the warmth of blood.
Seeking signs
instead of metaphors
and thus the single spot
where you are always to be found.
I'm on my way to translate anthills,
to taste tea with closed mouth,
to slice tomatoes
under the salt of verse.

2
Inviting Him In

The shame that the survivor is right,
set apart from judgment
and with the verdict's arrogance!

Who would gainsay
that the green is green?
It gives our words
a beautiful certainty,
the significance of solid ground.
But the composition
to which a heart is obliged
keeps its motif
like the Ammonite
at whom the dead man gazed.
He would extend feelers,
change vine leaves into spiralling ferns,
bring errors to bloom,
hear the autumn as the smell of snow.
But do not forget the houses
in which you live with us.
The lounge chair in the garden
will suit you fine
or the view of trees from the window
with you resting elbows on your knees.
Come in out of the rain and speak!

3
Conversing With Him

Here it did not begin and began,
here it is continued

in a rustling from the next room,
the click of shutters,
in shoes pulled off behind the door.
The pallor of your face that wipes out
color does not count.
Sentences grow out of habits
hardly noticed.
The manner of tying a cravat
becomes a decisive objection,
the ability to fall asleep quickly
a proof against your own interpretation,
the preference for tea
orders the beings of animals.

4
Finding His Theme

Interchangeable
the knocking at the door
with which the conversation began
and the signal as
the trolley rang its bell,
the name on the gravestone
and the name on the garden gate,
grown-up children
and post card greetings from Ragusa.

Words as weavings in the air,
the organ's voice out of its bellows,
the decision
to hear the song
or to be the song—
twisted uprights
as lines of descent for phosphorus
when the theme begins.

No variations tolerated,
not the evasions of power
nor the lulling truth brings,
cunningly
raising questions
behind the broad back of the answer.

5

Reading His Book and His Death

Figures settling
in the shut-down pits of Tin Forest
behind the demon states
of Mountain Chains and Seasons,
while the foreground
is occupied by bullies
who divide our time amongst themselves.

Pirna balancing the pyramids,
the freedom of long distance express trains
cashed into small change by block guards.
The ethnically grounded family
the scorn of nomads and individualists.

But objections raised
are turned back as eager adjectives
into the original sentence,
a train of termites
that hollows it
into a thin skin
of black letters.

Style is in dying,
the bullet in the bowels,

white rose of morphium dream,
the jesting at life meant seriously,
salvos in a snowstorm.

6

Winning Confidence from His Life

While you participate in reflections,
lead the conversation through your death,
collaborating on poems,
pick up pears
and view new landscapes
(—but gardening I
resist absolutely—)
all the while
Simone froze into a stone figure,
her imagined warmth
beneath the chill of tears.

She awaits moss,
the injuries rain brings,
creepers and bird lime.
Decomposed she will be warmed
into a life that we're going to share.
Patience!

PUNCTUATION MARKS

Have gone,
have gone like birds—
who went, who flew,
comma, chickens,
running birds, who went?

Have gone,
have swum like chickens—
sickly colored, down the ponds,
who went, who swam,
fish, strangers,
semi-colon, who went?

Have gone,
have flown like fish,
who went, who swam
who died,
chickens, unremarkable messengers,
question marks,
boundary crossers, who went?

DELAY

I have been there
and there,
could also have travelled there
or stayed at home.
You can learn to know the world
without leaving home.
I learned to know Laotse
earlier than Marx.
But the
social hieroglyphic
reached me in the left twinkle of an eye,
the right had already passed.

LONG POEMS

Normal
Tell him
to use the left for the fork
and the right for the knife.
One-armed doesn't count.

Precaution
Chestnuts are in bloom.
I take it as fact
but express no opinion.

Reliance
I know one
in Salonica who reads me,
and one in Bad Nauheim,
that's already two.

Quiet Mail for Every Year
I'll whisper the first of January in your ear,
pass it on, I'll wait.

Provisional Reply for Pitiful Trees
Acacias are irrelevant.
Acacias are sociologically insignificant.
Acacias are not acacias.

Paper Time
The arch-father preserves
documents and aquarelles
in cardboard rolls.
Chance to future researchers,
nevertheless wise foresight.

Contribution to the Dante Year
Chandler is dead
and Dashiell Hammett.
No matter to me,
hanging on to evil
I'll simply
read Dante.

Ode to Nature
We have our suspicions
as to trout, winter
and the speed of falling bodies.

Hart Crane
What convinces me
are the thin shoes, the
simple step over scholarship
and railing.

LANDSCAPE SCIENCE

One thing I know
about the rare dry lands,
my brother knows it,
my deaf mother.

There is nothing to hear,
there are no family
relationships, no
pretexts, no conceits.

Dry lands are
geological and serve life,
do not mourn the petrified,
do not sleep on the heart's side.

So they serve us
as camomile does,
on the sides of hills and
to be taken like dewdrops.

OLD POST CARDS

10
Why was the coffee
not drunk?
Despite the floods
we were sitting well,
had rented boats between
trees of the boulevard.
Why did the sugar
not dissolve?
Nothing came to a finish.
For what it's worth telling
there are the saucers, one
Charlotte, the cashier, and the
sadly sodden reeds.

HILDE DOMIN

Hilde Domin, born in 1912 in Cologne, was 39 years old and had been living in exile for 20 years when she wrote her first poem. The year was 1951, the place happened to be Santa Domingo. The poem was written in German; she later translated it into Spanish.

With this poem Domin began the exile's return—in the sense that she returned to active participation in her native culture, expressing her consciousness in its language. There were two separate attempts at an actual return before she settled down, more or less, in Heidelberg, the place where she began her studies, first in Law, later in Economics and Sociology.

The problem of the exile's identity has occupied much of her consciousness and is reflected in her writings. She writes as a German poet speaking to fellow Germans. In a letter to Nelly Sachs, the acclaimed "Jewish" poet and herself an exile, Domin asserts the use of her native language: "Language serves as humanity's memory . . . The remembrance of man consists of all languages. The poet keeps that remembrance living and vivid . . . This each poet can do with his own language. Ours happens to be German."

Although she spent so much of her life as an exile, Domin is as much concerned with the return-from, and the present, the "Hier" as she titled one of her recent collections of poetry. The contemporary poetic consciousness, she claims, is concerned with the "Doppelköpfigkeit jeder Erfahrung"—the ambivalence inherent in every judgment of experience.

According to Domin the poet's profession is truthfulness; he is neither a *yea* nor *nay*-sayer. He is automatically a resister, but inasmuch as he expects to be heard by others, he cannot be a total negator. Without the belief in the existence of those who understand his call, he would be unable to speak a single word.

For Domin every poem is a call against the subjection of man, and his collaboration, in turning the human into a function. The poems speak for a return to consciousness of a singular identity in a more and more anonymous society. In her poetry one senses a constant watch on those actions that threaten man's humanity.

(The translations were made in collaboration with the author).

LANDSCAPE IN MOTION

One must be able to leave
yet be like a tree:
as if the root stayed in the ground,
as if the landscape passed and we stayed firm.
Hold the breath
until the wind slows down
and the foreign air begins to circulate,
until the play of light and shadow,
of green and blue
reveals familiar patterns
and we're at home again
wherever it is
and can sit down and lean at rest
as if this were the grave
of our mother.

CAUTIOUS HOPE

White pigeons
in the blue of
burned-out windows
are wars made for your sake?

White string of pigeons
through the empty windows
across the meridian lines.
Like rose bushes on graves
carelessly you take what is ours.
On the stone washed with tears
you place your small nest.

We are building new houses,
pigeons,
the beaks of cranes tower
over our cities,
iron storks erecting nests for men.
We are building houses
with walls of cement and glass
on which your rose foot
cannot take hold.

We're cleaning out the ruins
and forget the extreme hour
in the dead eye of the clock.
Pigeons, we are building for you:
you will
nest in the smooth walls,
you will
fly through our windows
into the blue.

And perhaps there will be a few children
—and that would be much—
who will play
hide-and-seek beneath you
in the ruins
of our new houses,
the houses we are building day and night
with the tall cranes.

And that would be much.

TRAVELING LIGHT

Do not grow habits.
A rose is a rose.
But a home
is no home.

Reject the object-pet
wagging its tail at you
in the shop window.
It errs. You
do not smell of permanence.

One spoon is better than two.
Hang it around your neck,
you are allowed one,
because it's hard to ladle
hot soup with your hand.

Sugar would run through your fingers,
like consolation,
like wish
the instant of fulfillment.

You are allowed one spoon,
one rose,
perhaps a heart
and, perhaps,
a grave.

APRIL

The world smells sweetly
of yesterday.
Scents are lasting.

Open the window.
All springs
enter with this one.

A spring that is more
than green leaves.
One kiss holds all kisses.

Always this smoothly glazed
sky over the city
into which the streets flow.

You know winter
and pain
are not the killers.

The air today smells sweetly
of yesterday—
which smelled sweetly of today.

AUTUMN EYES

Press your body
close to the ground.

The earth
still smells of summer,
and the body
still smells of love.

But the grass
is turning yellow over you.
The wind is cold
and full of thistle seeds.

And the dream that haunts you
on shadow-feet,
your dream
has autumn eyes.

NOT TO BE STOPPED

Your own word
who will retrieve it,
the living
a moment ago unspoken
word?

Where the word flies by
grasses wither,
leaves yellow,
snow falls.
A bird may come back to you.
Not your word,
a moment ago unspoken
word into your mouth.
You send out other words
to catch it,
words with colored, soft feathers.
The word is quicker,
the black word.
It always arrives,
it never stops
arriving.

Better a knife than a word.
A knife can be blunt.
A knife often
misses the heart.
Not the word.

At the end is the word
always
at the end
the word.

SONG OF ENCOURAGEMENT II

You have long been chased
around the doorless walls
of the city.

You flee and scatter
the confused names of things
behind you.

Trust, this most difficult
ABC.

I make a small sign
in the air,
invisible,
where the new city begins,
Jerusalem,
the golden,
made of Nothing.

ARRANGING MANUSCRIPTS

In the wine cellar
of my poems.
I am growing light-headed
over you.

Behind the window panes
a large cloud
slowly sails
from curtain to curtain.

COLOGNE*

The sunken city
sunk
for me alone.

I swim
in these streets.
Others walk.

The old houses
have large new doors
of glass.

The dead and I
we swim
through the new doors
of our old houses.

*Cologne is the author's native city. (Editors note)

REMIGRATION

I am just unlearning
the value
of an empty
tin can.

I have just learned
to throw away a tin can
with which my friend Ramona
for her guest
with which my friend Ramona
for me
ladles water from the large clay vessel
in the corner of the huts
when I am thirsty
at the edge of the world.

I am just learning here with you
to forget the value
of an empty
tin can.

ANXIETY

I fear
this arrogance
this security
without security
of those who live near the gasometer
and hate lilacs.
Fingers
without fingertips
always in touch
producing
artificial
amazement
fishhearted
like fish in swarms
flitting
behind cue words.

It is true, I fear
the cathode
in the brain
the press of the button
by which the cock
(a cock in New York,
a cock in Frankfort)
crows
in the same instant.

DO NOT GROW WEARY

Do not grow weary
but gently
to the wonder
as if a bird should light
hold out your hand.

MESSENGERS

The messengers
come from afar
from the other side of the wall

barefoot
they come
the long way

in order to deliver this word.
One stands before you
in clothes from afar

he brings the word I
he spreads his arms wide
he says the word I

with this parting word
just now you looked at each other
he gives himself over

continues in you.

UNICORN

Joy
this most humble creature
this gentle unicorn

so softly
one does not hear it
when it comes, when it goes
my house pet
joy

when it is thirsty
it licks away
the tears of dreams.

ARS LONGA

The breath
in a bird's throat
breath of air
in the branches.

The word
like the wind itself
its holy breath
goes in and out.

Always the breath finds
branches
clouds
throat of birds.

Always the word
the holy word
in a mouth.

ABEL ARISE

Abel arise
it must be played again
daily it must be played again
daily the answer must lie ahead
the answer yes must be made possible
if you don't arise Abel
how shall the answer
the only significant answer
how shall it ever change
we can close all churches
abolish all law books
in all the languages of the globe
if only you rise
and make it unspoken
the first false answer
to the only question
that counts
arise
so that Cain says
so that he may say
I am your keeper
Brother
how could I not be your keeper
daily arise
that it may lie ahead
this yes I am here
I
your brother
so that the children of Abel
may no longer be afraid
because Cain will not be Cain
I am writing this
I a child of Abel
daily afraid

of the answer
the air in my lungs diminishes
as I wait for the answer

Abel arise
that there may be new beginnings
among all of us

The fires that burn
the fire that burns on the earth
shall be the fire of Abel

and at the missiles' tail
shall be the fire of Abel

IT'S NOT THAT

It's not that
we are revolved
from night to morning
to night
on a ball of which we know now
that it's blue
which we see revolve
it's not that
we hang head over heels in the void
we're used to that
it's not even
the conveyor belt to which we're glued
from the time of our fabrication in the womb
our packaging into
boxes of all sorts and sizes
together with others
and finally into the smallest
darkest
alone
the smallest solitary cell
as narrow as the womb and as windowless
we're used to that

Didn't somebody say
these people and those
are used to torture?

That's not it
we have long subscribed to all that
each night we sign our agreement
for the children of each night
the pact is made on the sheet
swaddling cloth
shroud

you are revolved on a blue ball
head over heels from light into dark
you don't notice it
nor the conveyor belt
from loneliness into loneliness
your hand full of ashes
that's not it
although it is this also
you forget it in fine weather
it is the smallest conveyor belt
that is not visible
that is not agreed to
that turns up daily

On the large funnel
down which we must all go
you are only nearer to the bottom
I'm still farther up near the rim
a guard said in the KZ
to the people still alive
men who dug their graves
before being shot he the rifleman
you're nearer to the bottom
how close we are nobody knows
that it revolves
it revolves
he was on top and pushed them down
with this consolation

PRECAUTIONARY MEASURES

Autumn is coming
we must put lions on the leash

No one will come too close to us
if we keep the right animals

Something larger than man
when standing on its hind legs

He who returns the dog's bite
who steps on the snake's head
who presses shut the alligator's eyes
he'll be all right

ECCE HOMO

Less than the hope in him

such is man
one-armed
always

Only crucified
both arms
wide open
the Here-I-Am

WORD AND THING

Word and thing
lay closely pressed
against each other
the same body warmth
in thing and word

BIRTHDAYS

1
She is dead

today is her birthday
this is the day
on which she
in this triangle
between the legs of her mother
was pushed forth
she
who pushed me forth
between her legs

she is ashes

2
Always I think
on the birth of a deer
the way it sets its legs on the ground

3
I've forced no one into the light
only words
words do not turn the head
they stand up
immediately
and walk off

MANY

Many lie there
I dip my hand in water
I touch the brow, the hair
of each,
the gentle curve of throat
when I touch the hair
it still smells
the dead man rises
he is almost in the room
then I touch your hair
it is his
there are hundreds
or you raise your hand you say something
one of them rises
the floor beneath me
changes
the sun changes
when they come
one of them
when his shape covers you
I touch his hair
when I touch yours

GRAY TIMES

It must be preserved
as if it came out of gray times

People like us we among them
sailed on ships back and forth
and could not land

People like us we among them
could not remain
and could not go

People like us we among them
did not greet our friends
and were not greeted

People like us we among them
stood on foreign shores
begging for pardon that we existed

People like us we among them
were spared

People like us we among them
People like you you among them
every one

can be undressed
made naked—
naked human dolls

more naked than animal bodies
beneath the clothes
bodies of victims

Undressed
who in the morning still had their shells about them
white bodies

Lucky he
who was only pushed
from pole to pole

Gray times
I speak of the gray times
when I was younger than you are now

I WANT YOU

Freedom
I want to
rough you up with emery paper
you, spit-polished

(the one I mean
mine
ours
freedom from and to)
Fashion mug

you are licked
with the tips of tongues
until you're fully round
ball
on all felts

Freedom word
I want to rough up
I want to dress up with glass splinters
so that it comes hard to take you on the tongue
and you're nobody's ball

You
and other
words I want to dress with glass splinters
As Confucius commands
the old Chinaman

A square bowl he says
must
have corners
he says
or the state will perish

nothing else, he says
is necessary
call
round round
and square square

THREE WAYS TO WRITE A POEM

1

A dry river-bed
a white row of pebbles
seen from afar
on this I want to write
in clear letters
or the mounds
of a refuse dump
slipping beneath my lines
sliding
so that the precarious life of my words
their nevertheless shall be
a nevertheless in each letter

2

Small letters
exact
so that the words come softly
so that the words creep in
so that one must go
to the words
look for them on the white
paper
softly
one does not notice how they enter
through the pores
sweat running into you

Fear
mine
yours
and this nevertheless in each letter

3
I want a strip of paper
as long as I am
a meter sixty
on it a poem
that cries
when someone passes by
cries in black letters
that demands something impossible
civil courage for example
the courage no animal has
pain-with for example
solidarity instead of herd
abstract words
made concrete through action

Man
animal with civil courage
Man
animal that knows pain-with
Man abstract-word-animal word-animal
Animal
that writes poems
poem
that demands the impossible
from each passer-by
urgently
not to be pushed aside
as if it called
"Drink Coca Cola"

ERICH FRIED

Born in 1921 in Vienna, Fried at the age of 17 left for London where he presently makes his home. His knowledge of the English language is such that he has been able to translate Dylan Thomas as well as Shakespeare into German. Nevertheless he continues to write as a German poet in the German language.

Fried speaks of himself as a German poet. In fact he considers his emigration in 1938 as a piece of literary luck insofar as he, on foreign soil, was able to come in touch with German expressionism more easily than others of his generation who did not leave home. He has said that perhaps with more talent and a greater willingness to adapt to a foreign culture he might have come to write English poems in German, or even in English, "but where poetry is generated in a man, he is rarely either capable or willing to adapt." Moreover, Fried claims, "every expression is an attempt to overcome Rilke's incontrovertible words that he who goes out never returns home."

If Fried has been influenced by English literary traditions it has not been through its lyric poetry. Of all the English poets, Auden with his interest in poetry as language, perhaps comes closest to Fried. Through Fried's ironic voice pompous language reveals its hollow other side. The voice tends to be rhetorical. The poet issues decrees; he scorns, he is mocking and often bitter. Brecht was perhaps his greatest influence.

All tyrants, and tyrannies are targets for his hard-hitting wit. His blasting humor serves a solid critical perspective.

AT THE REST STOPS

At the rest stops of war
stones open eyes
eyes open stones
rails sound peace

At the rest stops of war
on the stretch towards peace
the opened stone
is a chosen book
the picked up stone draws
the eye to that stretch

On the rails
dew and death
glitter
threshholds
swell with lethargy
stone hits steel and gives forth fire
steel hits stone and gives forth water
from burning eyes

INSCRIPTION

There where the mighty
listen to words of reason
there the wise are
just to one another
there stones swim
and save the drowning fish
there young and old
understand one another

DREAM TALK

I dreamed
my dream came

It said:
Time to start dreaming!

I looked at it:
What? You?

No, you!
Else there won't be any you.

RECURRENT DREAMS

Here I was placed
here
I was displaced
on the bridge
to a bridge
opposite the end
of a recurring dream

Time
no longer has time:
Here remains
what has preceded
here Death is
in play
and the game
is finished

Love meets its love
and can go no further
In sleep life comes
swimming into the net of sleep:
flying fish
that scare away the gulls
Here it is dry
waking up they burn

DEEP DREAM

My dream is a puzzle
a well over
which pears have grown
blonde pears
giving milk
and blood

Two possibilities:
Either civilization or the wild
In the well my mirror image
or the image of pears
Creation or exhaustion
a white and red glow

Are those heads
that think of danger?
Over frightened features
over fleeing brows
flowing strands
wave

Always her hair
always the salt of her vessels
that long
have gone to the well
and water it
with tears

HUMORLESS

Boys
in fun
throw
stones
at frogs

Frogs die
in all
seriousness

DEEDS

The smell is of something burning
even when one doesn't know what.
Freedom, so guarded now,
what will it smell like?

How will it look from above
or from inside
or from behind
in ten or twenty years?

How will one explain to children
that once one
let trees be poisoned
let children be burned?

And what will
the history books say
after his death?
With whom will they compare him?

BIRTH OF A MERMAID

At night the moon
sucks the sea to itself
flying fish and pond
and rocking boats

In the green-blue light
loose rowboats swim
with sailors and their brides
up into the sky

But the sky is high
a large scavenger fish is hungry
and begins to eat
the naked maiden in flight

At daybreak everything
falls out of the clouds
boats and bodies
crash on coastal cliffs

Besides the broken shipboards
next to the dead sailors
the bloody remains are found
half fish half woman

TWO LAUGHING SOLDIERS FROM ST. PAULI

If I had not learned from Saigon
that Sergeant Luong always giggled
as he faced the prisoners of war
whom he shot
I would not now
whenever I hear laughter
think of "Laughing Larry"*
and of Ky's words "My model is Hitler"**

If I had not learned
of what happened in Vietnam
my life would be easier
although some say
there's nothing you can do about it
and therefore it doesn't make sense
for you to spoil our joy in life
for us and for yourself

But when I resolve on silence
I see Sergeant Luong
and Air Force General Ky
here at home, with different names
to be sure, cleaning their teeth
in order to face us prisoners
with bright shining laughter

*"The nickname *Laughing Larry* was given Sergeant Luong by the Americans because of his habit of giggling as he shot Vietcongs," Saigon correspondant, Alan Williams in *Queen* London 7/20/1966
**I have only one model, Hitler," Marshall Ky, 7/6/65

LOVE SONG

The house must fall
the stream gnaws at the earth
the wind drives the sand away
on which the house is built

The wind drives the sand:
the way rustlers drive cattle
grains of sand complain
because the house must fall

The stream gnaws the earth:
the way rats gnaw in the cellar
crumbs of earth complain
because the house must fall

The house will not fall:
free of earth and sand
washed by the stream
dried by all four winds
foundation walls spread stone wings

DEFEAT

Where does war kneel?
where does it wait for forgiveness
full of humility on the dusty roads?
Reality

rides its hooves over fairy tales
lies saddle desire
to ride it once more to market
and again to shame

Wedding
of stallion and snake
what was that?
The dream stops

and in the waking nightmare I see
that post-war
is once more
pre-war

PAUSE

I hang my youth on the first gray hair
and my hope on the past:

To have come far
without advancing

Everything on one hair
and that hair grows gray
Everything on one day
and that day grows clouded

And in the fog
there is also my own gray dread:
I stand next to myself
and want to see my shadow
and pass the time with questions
of what is coming to me.
Shall I come to myself
or does it only seem that way in the fog?

Am I the eye of the fog?
the center of the torpid air?
A quiet place in the white wind
I don't know

Am I still able to loosen a kid's shoe laces
after so many steps?
And do I today truly
have more to say than to keep quiet
to teach than to perform?

Because it is not enough
to show discouragement
to lose oneself

and take refuge in complaints
Even a wise whine does not heal
and does not make holy
rather pesters
rather darkens
and slinks a whitish snake
the belt of fog
from one generation to the next

To have come far
and not advanced

The day hangs on a game
the game hangs before a mirror
eyes and heart hang who knows where
yet love hangs
on a hair
and that hair grays

And without love
one would have to cut
eye and heart from the trunk of time
remove without blessing
dark windows from their crosses
and lay them with the whitening
and lay them with the passing
here and there

TO THE WATERING HOLE

The tree lifts its roots out of the earth
and goes to the watering hole
Slowly it goes to the water
there animals lick their tears

The tree goes to the watering hole
Lightning strikes behind it
On the empty spot
the woodsman stands in surprise with his axe

The tree comes to the watering hole
it leaves its dead leaves
its worms creep after it
and die on the road

The tree comes to the watering hole
Its salt turns its wood to stone
Animals lick their tears
in its dead shadow

IN THE FOREST

Whether the forest was a fairy tale
whether I had ever been there
whether the tree tears its roots
out of the earth to go drinking

Whether my heart is bound in a shell
whether it hops in the branches
do I still remember
does it still stir my heart

When fire threatens all forests
all animals and children
when poison sprays
from the air curl leaves

defoliating trees
in their green time
so that rings of growth
and birds no longer count

The forest has long been surrounded
only I never saw it
in the green on the quiet road
that did not lead into quiet

(Note: This poem is a "counter-poem" to the previous "To the
Watering Hole". It was written in the sixties about ten years after the
first poem. Fried titled the collection: *"Befreiung von der Flucht—
Gedichte und Gegengedichte"* [Freedom from Flight—Poems and
Counter-Poems]. Editors Note.)

LOOKING BACKWARD

While men starved
I spoke
of ants
spiders and snakes

My despair
must have been
great

Now I speak
once more
against the death
of human beings

Has my despair grown
larger
or smaller?

DECREES

The lazy are to be executed
The world is to become industrious

The ugly are to be executed
The world is to become beautiful

The fools are to be executed
The world is to become wise

The sick are to be executed
The world is to become healthy

The sad are to be executed
The world is to become gay

The old are to be executed
The world is to become young

The enemies are to be executed
The world is to become friendly

The evil are to be executed
The world is to become good

GREAT SHIPWRECK

When freedom
flits
through gaps
like fish

and luck
runs along water
with birds
over fields

and justice
is weighed
in the scales
on sandy bottoms

I shall wipe
air bubbles from my mirror
in order to see myself
before drowning

THOSE WITH WORDS

I envy those with large words
they speak of the people
as if there were people
they speak of the fatherland
as if there were a fatherland
and of Love and Courage and Cowardice
as if all three existed
Courage Cowardice Love
and they speak of fate
as if there were a fate

And I'm amazed at those with sharp words
who speak of people
as if there were none
and of the fatherland
as if there were no fatherland
and of Love and Courage and Cowardice
as if it were clear
that none of these existed
and who speak of fate
as if there were no fate

And often I don't know
whom I envy and who amaze me
as if there were only amazement and no envy
or there was only envy and no amazement
as if there were only largeness but no sharpness
or there were only sharpness and no largeness
and then I no longer know whether
there are such things as speaking and knowing
or existence or my self
only that that's not the way it is

THE FREEDOM TO OPEN THE MOUTH

The freedom to open the mouth
exists even there
where others cry:
These mouths are to be shut!

So much so
one need only posit a list
of everything that may come
out of the mouths supposedly shut

First screams
second at the beginning
and finally at the end
perhaps even protests

Third teeth
and fourth blood and fifth
vomits
and sixth in many cases

liquids
that were first injected
through tubes or
through immersions of the head

One must not have a one-sided view
because the freedom to open the mouth
is an equal right for all
and certainly for the authorities as well

to open the hard-bitten mouth
of the prisoner
What to put in it?
Much water or much oil

or the heel of boots
or dirt and bloody rags
or urine
or sawdust or earth

so that there comes out of it
if everything works well
the freely willed
confession

Sometimes the mouth gets hurt
but there's always the freedom to open it
which will continue to govern—in one way or another—
throughout our land

HOPEFUL MISFORTUNE MESSAGE

With misfortune it is always assumed
that fortune
must be simple
and misfortune crooked and confused

It is unfortunate that misfortune
always muddles
the eye and robs vision
of its compelling form

Could we once see
the inner logic of misfortune
we would love
its classical features

free of crooked
confusing pre-judgments
That would be
misfortune's fortune

AN OLD MAN

As if thought could yawn
as if my yawn could
think mouth over head
of the time before fatiguing fear
    But the time still granted me
    yawns away
    torn wide open for coffins
    because again two have died

One of them the lucky guy
whom she loved
I went empty-handed
I stood there with open mouth
    Always hold hand
    over yawning mouth
    and close eyes
    The false teeth
    again misplaced

I saw her braids hang
in my dark glass hand
which I pass
over my eyes
    Propose
    "The past hangs on
    a thread of spit in yawning"
    Laugh at me

Her youthful face
trickles from my eyes
past the rims of the weaker spectacles
to the two dead
   Always cover your mouth
   when spit trickles or water
   and no one thinks any more
   that one can still think

WORLD TRAVELERS

Sounds of distant shores in their ears
are only harbor cries
and rattling of anchor chains
trembling of trains
arrival of heavy lorries
the screeching of beaten wives
and the funnel blasts
of ship sirens
at the passion time of a Christ-like sea voyage

And the smell of strange lands in their nose
is the sweat and dust
and half-smoked spices
and children's urine in damp quarters
and rot-gut
and city dust after summer rains
and hot walls in the evening
and polish and grease
and cheap whore perfume

And what they take as the color of cities
that hits their eye
is only the tarnished color
of poverty in old cities
and their boasts
of wide voyages
only means:
we have travelled far
in our misery

GROWING PAINS

In the first years
of reconstruction
there still remains
a deplorable
lack
of luxury goods

Beware:
What will then
be sold in the Co-op
for real wolf skin
used to be our black sheep
deceptively redone

THOUGHTS UNDER UNASSUMABLE CIRCUMSTANCES

Assumed
that dust together with bone splinters
could speak and said:
Assume
that in those last minutes
with the gas already coming
and the screams of children
ending in coughs and vomiting
I searched for
the precise formulation of that
which no one any longer hears

and finally assume
that you too cannot hear me dust
with bone splinters
not my formulation
yes not even
my invitation to assume
I had used
those last minutes
in successfully working out
the formulation

then you will know
how useless it is to make formulations
under circumstances
that take away everything
even the assumption
that dust can speak

POEM OF COMMITMENT

I remember
my anger
and my search
for the right words
for my anger
and the last revision
before the finished copy
and my reading aloud to myself alone
and lastly my
satisfaction
which took away my anger

And I may forget
how I snatched in vain
for the white sheets
and my fear
that my fingers
would become still more hopeless
because the carbon
had fallen to the floor
in front of the finished copy
and my head spun
as I picked it up

LYRICAL WINTER

Here too in the wet grass
between the better houses
where the grayish-white is perhaps already hoar frost
or still fog
and the smell of fungus lasts longer than fungus
in the mould under the ferns
here too nature exists and therefore
also nurture for poets
that grows with the mushrooms of which it smells
and is edible or not
depending on the recipe
no more poisonous than what you're used to
Then come and graze here

Come and feed on the green
in winter grass
you nobler ones
who kept your distance from medium sized feelings
against expensive wars
to be had cheaply

Be wise you smart one
Leave even the golden mean
to which you were loyal
and which shared its gold
with you, leave (it won't run away)
Come: the grass is dearer to you
Here you can have your nature! Here enjoy
the advantages of all those who are dragged along
believing themselves to hold the reins
Come: It is high time. Here you will regain
the old powers: Here see leaves fall
not suspicions. Here wake
from the stupefaction from which the pretended

free choice of deafness has insufficiently
protected you masters of hibernation
Here you can hear the grass grow
or see it fade and can trample the wind
or step on it in nature's sterile womb
lay windy eggs

Anything more gets thrown into the bargain

SPEECHLESS

Why are you
still writing
poems
knowing that
by this method
you accomplish
only small things

my friends ask
impatient that
their methods only
accomplish
small things

and I
have no answer
for them

ERRING COMRADES

True, Lenin is supposed to have said
"Only he who does nothing never errs"
but that was a long time ago
and one must not annoy those who are right
therefore no more mercy
for the erring comrades
and with those comrades
who showed mercy to the erring ones

But these too deserve advice:
Those who may still wander freely
are beginning to preach
loudly to those behind bars
one must be patient
and never mistake
will o' the wisps for shore lights
which is certainly true

and certainly each holds fast
to his own correct line
and at the most wonders
when his turn comes
but then he knows who's to blame
those erring comrades
who wanted to harm him
with their senseless disputes

END OF A CULTURAL EPOCH

The camp commander
a cultured man
made a finished copy
of his confession
improved
the wording and
here and there
inserted a jest

But no one laughed
and at the end he said
the future looks bad
for humor

NEW NATURE POETRY

He knows how boring it would be
if poetry were made only
of the contradictions of society
and that it would be better to write
of the pines at morning
so that immediately a poem occurs to him
on the necessity of changing themes
and his decision
to write of pines at morning

But even when he really gets up early enough
to be driven to the pines at morning
does anything occur to him of their image and odor?
Or does he catch himself on the ride thinking:
Should we get there
and they by chance have already fallen
to lie without branches on the sandy cliffs
between sawdust twigs and fallen needles
because some speculator has bought the land

That would be very sad
but then the smell of sap would be stronger
and the morning light on the sawed-off yellow stumps
would be brighter because no longer would
the crowns stand in the sun's way. This
would make for a new impression
and certainly more than enough
subjective experience
to allow for a poem
of accusation against this society

WINTER BIVOUAC

And the cheerful fires
where have they gone?
We who ask sit shivering
in twos and threes while
the cold shines bright
I'm beating my arms over my chest
I'm beating my chest over my heart
I'm beating my heart over my fear
layer over layer over layer
and inside
who knows?

An onion dragging out the winter
and the cold cuts and it must weep
The wise ones chew the hard ration with hard-bitten mouths
and the cheerful fires
where have they gone?

TRUE STORY WITH MORAL

On the 15th of January 1940 in Sweden
Bertolt Brecht proposed to a leftist actor
suggestions and directions
for de-moralizing:

"In the interest of the class struggle
should-and-ought sentences
containing the words 'you pig'
are to be changed

into propositions containing the words 'you ox' "—

that is
to be derived from profit and loss calculations
rather than from a morality gone sour

Thirty-three years
have since passed
and today comrades
in discussion

with comrades and others
are changing "you ox"
into the more forceful
"you pig"

and how this will serve the class struggle
no pig any longer asks

NOSTALGIA

Come back you play-actors

I take off my hat to your
jaunty wide brims
your visored caps
disheveled hair
come back
come
from your rained-out or
sand-covered graves
in the now still wilder West

Come back you directors of directors
come once more
with your marked cards
the ace up your sleeves
the tilted roulette
your hollow dice
filled with live mercury

The game is all for nothing
and when I was a child
it was for nothing
that one said "for honor's sake"
so then I knew: honor is nothing

you play-actors
have given up your honor
in order not to give up anything
you played it right
right up to the bloody *happy end* of your film

Once more indulge me
you forerunners!

How I long
for the simplicity of your tricks and small winnings
for the man-to-man battles to which cheating led

Windy great-grandfathers without air-conditioning
how you would stare at the tables that hold us today
bound to false moves
and which
heavily armed players play against us
according to rules that change
from card to card

On the wall it is written:
"Only he who fights is a man"
so that in all righteousness
they can shoot us down

GÜNTER KUNERT

Günter Kunert was born in 1929 in Berlin, a "mischling" —the Nazi term for children of racially mixed parentage. He was 16 when the war ended and many of the poems continue to bear witness to this traumatic period. Kunert remains a citizen of the D.D.R. and a socialist, but was expelled from the Communist Party in 1974 after signing a petition in support of Wolf Biermann, the dissident balladeer exiled from his native East Berlin.

One senses an humanistic warmth in Kunert's poetry. His sensibility is alert to threats against the free individual. It is not only to fellow Germans that Kunert addresses himself. The "Signs—Berlin Style" are shared by all contemporary cities where a "lost bird flies" in the "zealously created wastes": Nagasaki, Detroit, Warsaw, etc. Kunert has been called a literary rarity .. a poet repected and established in both East and West Germany.

Besides revealing a social consciousness the poetry tells what it is to live existentially with knowledge of death. Brecht and Kafka are both influences. Kunert's dialectic often concludes in absurdity: resolution is rare. The despair has a touch of the bizarre and an existential foundation Kunert shares with Kafka. Someone has spoken of the "steely softness" of his lines.

"The purpose of a poem," Kunert has written, " is its reader, who, while he is engaged with the poem, finds himself necessarily engaged with himself: in a dialectical process which the poem prescribes and exemplifies at the same time."*

---

*"Paradoxie als Prinzip" (Paradox as Principle) in *Warum Schreiben* (Berlin und Weimar 1976)

"Hausvisite" (House Calls) is a poetic expression of the joined individual and social consciousness. In the poem, writers, tyrants, hypocrites, history, clichés "call" and make their presence felt. Then they go, and what remains is the inexorable passage of time. But Kunert does not leave us in despair. The last poem in *Warnung Vor Spiegeln* (Warning of Mirrors) is "Vorschlag" (Proposal): Ram the rod, he says, place your mark there, a "secret memorial of your once upon a time presence." And this is what his poetry is doing.

HOUSE CALLS

Days come, days go,
here comes a knock at the door, the bell rings,
here comes Ferlinghetti, he brings a waxen
rose: stolen
from the compost behind the memorial where
yesterday's wreaths are bedded for their final rest
where remembrance rots and faded ribbons capitulate
before a world which is running down screeching.
Giant alarms
that wake no one, that only ring and clang:
Here comes a further analyst of incontrovertible truth
Mao, the masked dragon, chameleon
of many colors, chews a thousand blossoms, beats
on his bag: millionaire,
pays everything in pure living souls, generous,
but with a bad memory when asked
whether
he does not remember the mustache
he once wore: Because days have come and days have gone:
Fell, banged shut behind you, gates
of castles, castles bolted shut: Vitality
reduced to submissive rattlings,
gymnastics for a
rained out Sunday afternoon.

But
days come as friendly visitors to those
who promise to live in each one of them,
who take the eternal present as a daily event and swear
never to betray it to tomorrow and its
powerless majesty.

But
he who comes, who sticks when despite everything

more is yet to come: Man
whose home has no other dimension
than the present:
Everything will be done now or never,
that which was not done will come back.
Here comes Dr. Luther and says: Freedom now.
Here come parallel lines meeting sometime
in infinity: but when will
infinity get here?
Here comes
an old, dusty-bearded, truly-gruesome
Something
that raises its hand and speaks: Our children
will one day have a better life!
But:
what is better for them nobody knows better
than they themselves at the time,
because days that come are different from those
that go, that knock on the door, on bars and shutters.
Hide, call out, crawl under the bed:
Punctually there arrives
the 24 hour sphinx, shows her naked breasts,
shows claws: tame her
or be devoured!
But in any case spare all those with instructions for lay lion tamers
who lust after the tempting and deadly
day
wanting nothing of doses of time to be used shortly

Because both wax and living roses
grow out of stone and dirt,
Ferlinghetti arrives, Mao arrives, the Dioscuri arrive,
antagonists arrive, and of all these there

remains only that
which moves without interruption into the present, because days
will not be stopped.

THE LAST HOUSE

On the right a high barbed-wire fence.
Already rusted. Grown over with weeds
at the foot. At the left low-lying houses. Close
as close. Old, a hundred years or more.

The last house on the street:

reddish and raw, naked
crumbling brick, a wing without windows
closes the street
with finality. There

in a dream I found myself. There I stood
before the small double door made of lead
only leaning shut, and opened it: went
bowed in the narrow space perspective made
up to the next leaden doorway, this time
harder to open. Two old men
appeared: the only ones
to survive the mass murders,
hidden behind leaden doors, protected
by the last decaying house, invisible
in the windowless wing: they cried

because it had taken 25 years
for my dream to find them.

I CALL STOP THIEF!

Just now with new hat and white shirt
hair beneath hat, heart beneath shirt,
before the mirror, scarcely
turning about I call:
Stop Thief! the hat
is gone like hair, like shirt, heart.

Unnoticed, faceless he comes
in many masks, measurable but
not to be grasped, carries it all away

Sometimes I'm horrified at
his traceable, sudden proximity:
Stop Thief! I cry: He
is taking my life!
But he runs on, he speeds, runs
and races and with ever increasing hurry
carries millions of hats and millions of hearts
towards nowhere.

BERLIN AFTERNOON

In summer with a clouded sky
in summer with a soft rain
in summer in the cool of old dwellings
between the pregnant forms of dark wallpapers:
there to lie
and listen to the inter-urban train
muffled door thumps
trotting horse carriages
staccato of hand driven machines
in wind blown backyards
the mortal play of wasted bodies
faint in the pale of secret beds
hidden behind crumbling fragments
behind scurfy growth of old houses
which suddenly one afternoon
shovels and cranes will lift
together with contents unceremoniously
without wreaths out of existence
into our memories where their passage, greeted and
grieved, comes to rest:
in summer
with a soft rain

THE OTHER SIDE OF THE STYX

Black waters seemingly
still. Points of light from dulled lanterns
running off in wavering mirror.
The other side is the other side. House silhouettes
without recognizable windows, something like burst
towers, shattered churches
shadowing the inky heavens over there.
There are no stars there. The other side is the other
and here is here and the boat crossings
long established. The stream: a flowing
border. No field glasses strong enough
to see whether anything is moving in the opposite shade
other than the hairy tailed shore inhabitants
multi-footed hordes of execution.

No sound. The quiet becomes a presence
and hums in one's ears; soundless trumpets
through which the stink of rotting waters
presses.

Morass holding no footprints:
what size shoe did Cain wear, or Abel?
Step into their tracks wherever we go.
Wherever—at the end it leads to this shore where
looking at this viscous and oily stream
the recognition dawns it's name is not
Thames, not Arno, not Seine, not Danube
not Spree

To learn its true name one crossing
is sufficient. But he who crosses
the stream
will be presented on the other side with the bill
for all the wrongs committed
of which he knew nothing.

Go, leave the black waters,
the lamplight that brightens nothing, go
and retreat
into the deafening din of city settlements,
home into the snail-shell before
over there the ferry begins its trip.

ROMANTIC POEM

There where he is at home
with a friendly greeting from an old dog,
his half-ear cocked listening, and the cat
without claws,
beneath the moon, sharpened to a cutting scythe
above,
below
dissolved in watery salt ponds in
the black harbor, while
something moves about, me, unreal past
the real houses of Lutow,
over the post office at Wolgast,
and a star drops unceasingly,
the man of the house considers his life,
the years between Moscow and Tula,
the words exchanged with the Kollontai,
toasted at Kalinin, at morning hope,
at evening fear, sawed-off dreams through the woods
from which returned home
to this place on the gently curved earth:
still to come to a resolution
greeted by cat and dog.

SOMETIMES SMOKE

rises from sewer manhole covers.
A window closing on a distant
house front is sometimes
announced
by a flash of light.
Sometimes the telephone rings
and the ear receives silence.
Sometimes echoes of salvos.

Messengers
still reach us: incomprehensible
as truth.

Sometimes
we stumble and fall
over the bones of the innocent:
rutted roads
from yesterday to today
through the swamp of the flowering present.

THE WAY

1

Trembling we hide
in well-lit caves from
the great darkness.
It comes so soon. Hardly come to life
it is ready to leave us. And before
we fully know it:
that strange wild pleasant It

2

Pulled together
in the soft womb of a woman
from never exhausted chemicals
this comglomerate creeps into the light
pulls himself up only to
bow down again

3

A little warmth gives bliss. The view
of the mountain top raises
the man standing before it in his own eyes. Between
the thighs of willing women convulsed
he forgets the black Nothing towards
which he hurries with every sigh, every
heartbeat, tick tock of clock, killing
hours, tens of years
and more than these

4

The puzzle is solved: there was none
Existence is disclosed and now called
never-been

5

He who moves from his bed into the grave
arrives nowhere. What
becomes of him
in books memorials aeroplanes monuments
in the memory of those who may still
put one leg before the other is no longer he:
all these
his accomplishments
he himself faded, blown in the wind, faded

6

That is the way
no signpost shows another. It leads
into darkness of which we
keep silent day after day. For we must daily
forget it all over again

TRICKERY OF ENEMIES

A Japanese company
on the island of Ioa
heard nothing
of the end of the war, of the silence
of weapons, of the exchange of wounded,
the freeing of prisoners, the start of construction
of wrecked houses and cities, but the next day
went on guard, spied behind each bush
startled by the cry of wild deer, distrustful
of the nightingale, whether it might not be
a disguised signal, guarded,
sleepless, completely worn out and believing
since no enemy came this a special
trick of the enemy

SCHILLER'S BED

Schiller's bed rests in the Schiller House
of the Goethe town. Tourists stand before the bed:
We want to be, don't know what, respectful
at least, if not more, master of the shameful yawn,
tired before this narrow resting place, too small
for my friend Reinhard,
his lean body lies, linen jacket
and glasses removed,
now
lying slack in the Grünewald woods
growing into earth, in this wise
following Schiller.

We wish to be somehow at one, not out of one egg.
Not twins. Not German Siamese.

Before this little bed, this paling cover, faded
wreath, the little ribbon, we do not
become what we never were: a unified people.

A people out of a few lordly masters, many
menials, related like hawk and chicken.

But Lettau in Berlin and I in Berlin
are brothers
along with those
condemned to wake out of the William Tell dream.

PROPOSAL

Ram the rod
into time shooting away from you.
Sand runs through your hand
shaping formlessness,
immediately to sink into itself
and never to be seen again:
a wasted life

What you did not create that
you are not. Your being only an equation
for being active: How will he
who does not build steps
go beyond himself?
Who will come home to himself
without companions of the road?

Leave behind more than a trace
of your paw, the testament
of extinct beasts of which the world
has seen more than enough

Ram the rod. Ram
a single, new thought
as a secret memorial
of your once upon a time presence
in the dyke
against the eternal flood

POOR CONSOLATION

1

Not to have discovered gunpowder.
The mystery of life unsolved,
a stretch of microcosm observed
with no way of knowing: is it going up or down
for either way it must go,
it is a curve which demands faith:
believe down, believe up

2

But for the discoverers of gunpowder
as well as for the solvers of the mystery of life
the conclusion reads:
No life after its passing,
none in name, none in word, none
in any name,
whether down or up, none at all:
scientific fact, that alien good which is always with us.

3

On a rainy afternoon
under the burden of mortality
sigh and moan
for that which rushes past the window
roaring like Niagara and not to be detained:
life: incomprehensible and meaningless

4

No less for the discoverers of gunpowder.

144 / Günter Kunert

INTROJECTIVE POEM

Wooden stairs: old decaying
endless often degraded Ancients
hierarchically layered
creaking in unchanging series
from below to above or
from above to below
depending on the climb: joined
by railings: polished privilege
on turned rods
lovingly grasped
while stairs must take each
step.

Legendary
that once all were
one and the same trunk.

DAYS AND DAYS

Days of weakness, days
of despair, days of blackness,
of pressure, all blows of the hammer,
whether near or far, striking you.
Death arrives like a newspaper:
where you find your sentence
officially announced:
A war is being waged against you,
the army of your friends is already marching,
ovations are projected,
honors. Orders. Laurels threaten,
goodness compacts, humanity is
running over:
even the weather has turned
against you: the sun shines
for you alone.

Sentence: It will not be forgiven you
that all the others may read it
on your face.

BITTER POEM

Refuge behind refuge
where did I read that
or experience it. Existence shows itself
mixed
with reality now and again and against
knowing better and the best of wills.

For example I exist
more as image in other men's
heads than in my own
as contents of a file box
perhaps official. There I am
not the same
as in my bed and not the same
as fastened in a seatbelt over the Atlantic
where things are unreal as in life.
I am not the same
when I am dead and when I am
not dead

living

I wash my hands
and beg for innocence
would like to be freshly free of blame
wipe the blood from me
full consequences of daily deeds
of which in reality we
know nothing more than what we read
or
whatever was made public
on our backs.

Happiness daily spilled

returns
out of the tears and folds
of the night.

In the dark it creeps
into the light of dreams:
tender, vulnerable and not to be stayed

for that reason first known as:

The Great Unknown
The Eternal Loss
The Painful Absence

A solitary
out of poetisized Never-Ever Land.

GLANCE IN THE MIRROR

Skin gritty and grayed.
The bearer misshapen:
Time crooks the verticals.

Abyss of all folds:
pointing to bottomless depths.
On the cranium: erosion:
bare cliff: porous: thoughts
pressing through, crooked, curling
in the dying fire:
Hephaistos going into a retirement home
with the stiff-legged walk of history.
How time runs: in panic, tired.

Fossils, before the museum swallowed them
were once life-loving animals,
young as their world was young,
or so it seemed to them.

THE RUSTLING OF RAIN

The rustling of rain on the window glass
in an old Berlin backyard
irregular yet urgent
incomprehensible Morse code

while you (which is how
I address myself in poems
but also you Not—I)
lie in an old Berlin bed
dark wood and feather quilt
and repeat old dreams

Perhaps
the rain falling in an old Berlin
backyard—
in between your life—
"Only a quarter hour."
And perhaps 50 people: all
you yourself, all me
and easily rained out as in old films
in repeated recollection

THE NEIGHBOR

She opens the hen cage
and does not know that once
in transport to market
across the ocean to New Orleans
ten million black-skinned people
simply died of starvation

Peoples flamed up and died out.

The destruction of masses
of neighbors behind the next corner
does not reach her and if:

she would not believe it and forget
the unbelievable. Bowed over beds
of cabbage and strawberries
behind her back whole communities
plunge into the ditch

which she and they one for the other
as well as each for himself dug

SIGNS—BERLIN STYLE

These don't set wings to fantasy
as their predecessors:
the torn down houses.
These stepped on the city stage,
their shabbiness hardly veiled by day,
their windows
dots of light on a black ground
each one repeating a nightly promise
of shining singularity: You behind them
unique content
you, secret terror of a secret lust
dust covered behind gray curtains
my life and you stranger's life
for one preys on the light and reflection
of the other: my bed companion
was a shadow running off
a naked lamp my torture
an empty cage my hope
a sudden extinction of light my end:
barren autumnal wallpaper
betrayed the city's history to me
damaged stones at the arched gates gave
philosophical advice
and the pattern of rain
on extinct facades taught me
art and the art of recognition:
between the streets of Nagasaki and Detroit,
Warsaw and Rotterdam, extending
to the Alexander Platz in Berlin, in the
zealously created wastes, a lost bird
unable to fly.

BERLIN DANCE OF DEATH

Cemeteries without towns surrounding them
show a certain over-abundance:
placed there in the landscape
they're a proof we can afford death:
we have enough bodies
to fit out any neighborhood
and rather
than suffer a lack, we shall cover
the whole earth
with a bleached layer of bones
over which small bunches of hair wave
when the wind moves: on our voyage
through the universe
in the direction of the forgotten Law
before which we shall spread our bones
and
beg for mercy.

REMEMBERING IV (for Christopher Middleton)

The blind one, named Memory,
distinguished by nothing more
than her name, this blind one brings
treasures, inaccessible and costly.

Gold has been made out of lead
to the surprise of alchemists; they
succeeded only in changing
men into inhabitants, peoples
into words, houses into boxes,
cities into deserts, in which
inhabitants of boxes appear in and out
according to the directions of words, without knowledge of
for what, where to, why.

A blind one, named Memory
raises her lid a crack. As
she looks at you without seeing you
you catch sight
of your birth in the sea's carbon layers.

And that you have long lost your secret:

For you have become visible, which is to say:
useful.
That your future fades along with images
of the future and has always been lost.
That you are at best an idiot. If not
simply
a rotation spun off from matter
for the generation of matter. Thus similar
to a godhead which because
of a lack of believers prays to itself,

who hires hordes of murderers,
who cannot bear the blind look
that has seen everything.

CONJUNCTIVE DOUBLE (for Peter Huchel)

Washed by rain
whitened by crows
visited by lizards
so would I stand.

My unrecognizable shoulders
burdened with day and night:
I'd place my faith in that.
Winds rubbing themselves raw
on my surfaces. At times
a glitter passing out from me
and the minute pincers
of insects writing their memoirs
on me.

Inside and outside
fully the same
insofar as no contemporary of time
which shall first recognize its existence in me
from my face as weather-beaten
as I am throughout.

I would be truth
but frozen
at sight of myself.